CHICKASAW

Big Buddy Books
An Imprint of Abdo Publishing
abdopublishing.com

Katie Lajiness

abdopublishing.com

Published by Abdo Publishing, a division of ABDO, PO Box 398166, Minneapolis, Minnesota 55439.
Copyright © 2017 by Abdo Consulting Group, Inc. International copyrights reserved in all countries. No part
of this book may be reproduced in any form without written permission from the publisher. Big Buddy Books™
is a trademark and logo of Abdo Publishing.

Printed in the United States of America, North Mankato, Minnesota.
062016
092016

THIS BOOK CONTAINS
RECYCLED MATERIALS

Cover Photo: © Peter Turnley/Corbis; Shutterstock.com.
Interior Photos: ASSOCIATED PRESS (p. 27); © Blue Lantern Studio/Corbis (p. 23); © Nancy Carter/North Wind
    Picture Archives (p. 9); *Getty Images*: MIGUEL MEDINA (p. 29); © Heritage Image Partnership Ltd/Alamy
    (p. 21); © iStockphoto.com (pp. 11, 15, 26, 30); © NativeStock.com/AngelWynn (pp. 5, 13, 16, 17, 25);
    Shutterstock.com (p. 19); © Christine Whitehead/Alamy (p. 21).

Coordinating Series Editor: Tamara L. Britton
Graphic Design: Adam Craven

Library of Congress Cataloging-in-Publication Data

Lajiness, Katie, author.
    Chickasaw / Katie Lajiness.
Description: Minneapolis, MN : ABDO Publishing Company, 2017. | Series:
    Native Americans
LCCN 2015050488 | ISBN 9781680781977 (print) | ISBN 9781680774924 (ebook)
LCSH: Chickasaw Indians--History--Juvenile literature. | Chickasaw
    Indians--Social life and customs--Juvenile literature.
LCC E99.C55 L34 2017 | DDC 976.004/97386--dc23
LC record available at http://lccn.loc.gov/2015050488

Contents

Amazing People. 4

Chickasaw Territory 6

Home Life 8

What They Ate. 10

Daily Life 12

Made by Hand 16

Spirit Life 18

Storytellers 20

Fighting for Land. 22

Back in Time. 26

The Chickasaw Today 28

Glossary 31

Websites 31

Index 32

AMAZING PEOPLE

Hundreds of years ago, North America was mostly wild, open land. Native American tribes lived on the land. They had their own languages and **customs**.

The Chickasaw (CHIH-kuh-saw) are one Native American tribe. They are known for their beautiful handcrafts and hunting skills. Let's learn more about these Native Americans.

Did You Know?

Chickasaw is a Muskogean name meaning to "sit down."

Today, young members of the Chickasaw tribe still practice their traditional dances.

5

CHICKASAW TERRITORY

Chickasaw homelands were in what is now northern Mississippi and Alabama. Over time, they spread to present-day Arkansas, Kentucky, Louisiana, Missouri, and Tennessee.

CHICKASAW HOMELANDS

MISSOURI

KENTUCKY

TENNESSEE

ARKANSAS

MISSISSIPPI

ALABAMA

LOUISIANA

CANADA

UNITED STATES

MEXICO

N
W — E
S

7

Home Life

The Chickasaw lived in villages. Some had more than 200 homes! To remain comfortable throughout the year, the Chickasaw built homes for both the winter and summer.

They built summer homes out of thin pieces of wood. These homes kept them cool and dry. And, they were rectangular in shape.

Winter homes were built in the shape of a circle. They were made with clay and grass. So, they were warmer than the summer homes.

Most Chickasaw summer homes had grass-thatched roofs.

What They Ate

The Chickasaw were skilled farmers, fishermen, hunters, and gatherers. Corn, beans, and squash were common crops. They also hunted deer, buffalo, and bears.

Chickasaw often searched for foods such as wild strawberries and nuts. They made tea from different wild roots and spices.

Chickasaw men hunted deer. Women cooked the meat in clay pots.

Daily Life

Chickasaw villages were long and narrow. Some were six miles long! Each village had a chief. **Ceremonies** were held in a home in the center of the village.

Men wore **loincloths**. Women wore deerskin dresses. In cold weather, they put on bear or buffalo-fur coats and deerskin moccasins. They had deerskin leggings to protect their legs when they rode horses.

Men's buckskin shirts were decorated with beads. The beads were sewn into tribal patterns.

Chickasaw men spent much of their time fishing and hunting. And, they traded with neighboring tribes and the British. At one time, the Chickasaw controlled all trade in the area.

Women were respected, owned land, and had authority in their communities. They gathered fruits and farmed many types of vegetables. And, women made clothes for their families. Children learned these skills from adults.

Chickasaw men used stone tools such as arrowheads to hunt and fish.

Made by Hand

The Chickasaw made many objects by hand. They often used natural materials. These arts and crafts added beauty to everyday life.

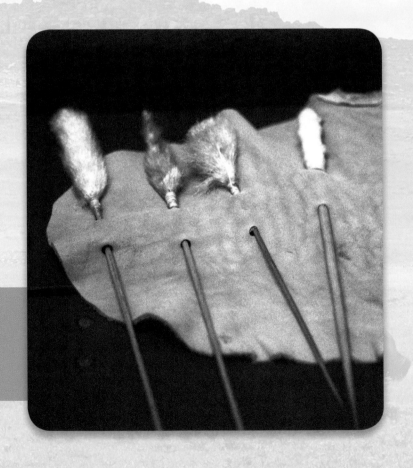

Blowgun Darts

Chickasaw made blowguns out of hollow cane. Darts were crafted from rock. Men used these tools to hunt small animals.

Rattles
Rattles were made from turtle shells, gourds, and cow horns.

Game Sticks
Chickasaw played a game with wooden sticks and balls made from deerskin.

Drums
They made ceremonial drums by stretching buckskin over gourds.

Spirit Life

Long ago, a priest called a *hopaye* led **ceremonies** and explained the meaning of signs and dreams. The Chickasaw's god was connected to the sky, sun, and fire. Their **rituals** were closely tied to the moon. The tribe also believed in witches and evil spirits.

The Chickasaw believed in life after death. They buried their loved ones facing west, so the dead could travel to a new world. In the 1800s, some of the Chickasaw became **Christians**.

The sun is an important spiritual symbol to the Chickasaw. To them, it represents heaven, rebirth, and the giver of life.

STORYTELLERS

Stories are important to the Chickasaw. Adults shared ancient stories to teach children about their tribe and **traditions**. Their creation story tells of two brothers who carry a magical pole that leads them to their homelands.

Some Chickasaw stories tell of floodwaters covering the whole world. In one story, a Chickasaw family and two of every animal survive a great flood. After the flood, a raven gives the Chickasaw corn to plant.

Other cultures have flood stories too, such as that of Noah and the Ark.

FIGHTING FOR LAND

Long ago, the Chickasaw were known as brave fighters. In 1540, Spanish explorer Hernando de Soto met the Chickasaw tribe. The Spanish forced the Chickasaw to give them food and housing. The Chickasaw fought for their freedom. The Spanish were afraid, so they left the area.

In 1786, the Chickasaw and the US government signed the **Treaty** of Hopewell. This agreement established a smaller area for the Chickasaw to live.

Hernando de Soto was the first explorer to meet the Chickasaw. He wanted to claim what is now Florida for Spain.

In 1830, the US Congress passed the Indian Removal Act. It forced the Chickasaw to live on Indian Territory in what is now Oklahoma. They had to share the land with other tribes. Some of these tribes were their enemies.

By 1920, about 75 percent of Chickasaw lands had either been sold or rented to settlers. Many Chickasaw moved away.

The US government forced the Cherokee, Chickasaw, Choctaw, Creek, and Seminole from their homelands. These tribes had to travel on what is now known as the Trail of Tears.

Back in Time

1856

The Chickasaw formed their own nation. They wrote a **constitution** and made laws. And, they established a **capital** city called Tishomingo.

1698

The Chickasaw first met the British. Explorers later built trading posts near tribal lands.

1865

After the **American Civil War**, settlers began to move onto the Chickasaw's land.

1906–1907

The US government put an end to the Chickasaw Nation and other tribes. The following year, Oklahoma became a US state.

1970

Congress again granted the Chickasaw tribe the right to elect its own leaders.

2010

The Chickasaw Cultural Center opened in Sulphur, Oklahoma, to educate others about the tribe's history and culture.

THE CHICKASAW TODAY

The Chickasaw have a long, rich history. They are remembered for fighting off the Spanish and for their bravery against enemies.

Chickasaw roots run deep. Today, the people have kept alive those special things that make them Chickasaw. Even though times have changed, many people carry the **traditions**, stories, and memories of the past into the present.

Did You Know?

In 2011, there were about 49,000 Chickasaw.

In 2015, Chief Phil Lane Jr. played a traditional drum during the Climate Summit near Paris, France.

"We never had a thought of exchanging our land for any other … fearing the consequences may be similar to transplanting an old tree, which would wither and die away."

– Levi Colbert,
   Chickasaw leader

GLOSSARY

American Civil War the war between the Northern and Southern states from 1861 to 1865.

capital a city where government leaders meet.

ceremony a formal event on a special occasion.

Christian (KRIHS-chuhn) a person who practices Christianity, which is a religion that follows the teachings of Jesus Christ.

constitution (kahnt-stuh-TOO-shuhn) the basic laws that govern a group of people.

custom a practice that has been around a long time and is common to a group or a place.

loincloth a simple cloth worn by a man to cover his lower body.

ritual (RIH-chuh-wuhl) a formal act or set of acts that is repeated.

tradition (truh-DIH-shuhn) a belief, a custom, or a story handed down from older people to younger people.

treaty an agreement made between two or more groups.

WEBSITES

To learn more about Native Americans, visit **booklinks.abdopublishing.com**. These links are routinely monitored and updated to provide the most current information available.

INDEX

American Civil War **26**

arts and crafts **4, 13, 16, 17**

Britain **14, 26**

Cherokee **25**

Chickasaw Cultural Center **27**

Choctaw **25**

clothing **12, 13, 14**

Colbert, Levi **30**

Creek **25**

farming **10, 14**

fighting **22, 28**

fishing **10, 14, 15**

food **10, 11, 14, 22**

France **29**

government **26, 27**

homelands **6, 20, 22, 24, 25, 26**

homes **8, 9, 12, 22**

hunting **4, 10, 11, 14, 15, 16**

Indian Removal Act **24**

Lane, Chief Phil, Jr. **29**

language **4**

religion **18, 19, 20**

Seminole **25**

Soto, Hernando de **22, 23**

Spain **22, 23, 28**

stories **20, 21, 28**

Tishomingo **26**

trading **14, 26**

Trail of Tears **25**

Treaty of Hopewell **22**

United States **22, 24, 25, 27**